AF252051

Talking Colors:
Seeing Words / Hearing Images

by Sandra Indig

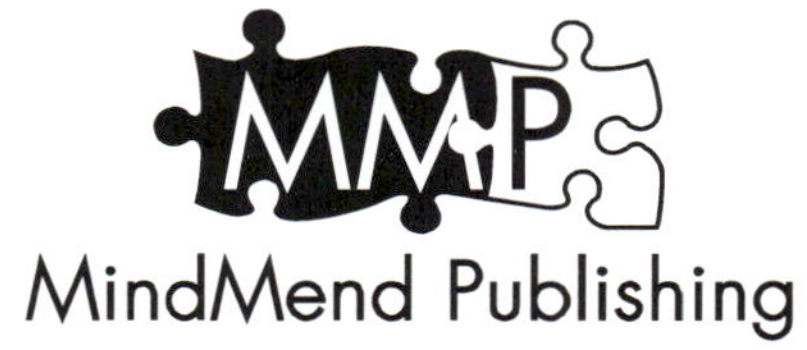

MindMend Publishing

Published in 2016 by the MindMend Publishing Co., New York, NY
Copyright © 2016 by Sandra Indig

All rights reserved

For permissions to reproduce any portion of this publication, email to ORIPressEditor@Gmail.com or write to MindMend Publishing Editor @ 7515 187th Street, Fresh Meadows, NY 11366.

Printed in the United States of America on acid free paper.

Library of Congress Control Number: 2016963580

Cataloging Data:
Indig, Sandra. Talking Colors: Seeing Words/Hearing Images / Sandra Indig.

1. Poetry-Psychological aspects. 2. Art-Psychological aspects. 3. Unconscious communications.
4. Religion-Psychological aspects. 5. Spirituality-Psychological aspects.

ISBN-13: 978-1-942431-06-0 (soft cover)

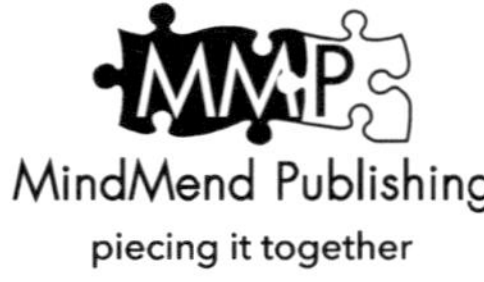

Book design, editing, and book cover - by MindMendMedia, Inc.
@ MindMendMedia.com

This book is dedicated

to my inheritance

and

to my grandmother Dora

Table of Contents

Publisher's Preface

"The feeling of pain resembles the anguished, troubled height of convulsions, and suffering-the long and the slow kind – has the intimate yellow which colors the vague bliss of profoundly felt convalescence" (Fernando Pessoa)

MindMend Publishing of New York City is pleased to announce the publication of *Talking Colors: Seeing Words/Hearing Images* by Sandra Indig. The first encounter with this book brings the association with synesthesia, a condition of "cross-talking" of otherwise separated senses. Each page is like an illuminated manuscript where words and images, pain and bliss often blend into an other-worldly whole. The author's sensibility is the result of a cross-pollination of multiple disciplines: art, poetry, psychoanalysis, and dance. The immediate stimulant for the distillation, cohesion and transformation of a life time of study and practice culminated with the author's focus on ancient Hebrew texts and study of Torah.

Indig does not take credit for her words and images but, instead, insists that they are presented as gifts. She maintains that both responsibility and credit for her productions are hers but not the form or words in which they initially appear. She also disputes the easy description of abstraction. Neither her words nor her images are abstractions but rather they are presentations from a source which cannot be understood or grasped through the mind alone. Perhaps, like the surrealists, the author paints and talks about what is behind the veil of the observable, conscious mind, or identifiable world of objects.

Like Viktor E. Frankl in his *Man's Search for Meaning*, Sandra Indig holds with the notion that, if we are lucky, we create our own realities, our own meaning. Through her work, Indig grasps the Kabbalistic concept of *tikkun olam*, defined by acts of kindness and our responsibility for repairing what is broken; of healing the soul/self and of mending the world through deeds performed.

Many thanks to Sandra Indig for trusting us with producing this book, and for sharing her wisdom, creativity, and her talent of connecting seemingly unconnected domains.

MindMend Publishing Staff

Author's Preface

Caught in the Grip of Words/Images

Words/Images are places to which one goes to live or to die again and again. They are personal attempts to concretize the meaning of exploratory, unspoken thought. Words/Images, like gestures in dance, unlock associations, connections, and transform the way it was to the way it will be. They create the us-to-be.

In Treatment

I have seen eight compulsions in the form of: secrets, erasures, obfuscation, denial, rationalization, cover-ups, hiding, and burying, all racing toward three gates of hell: shame of exposure, fear of humiliation, and guilt.

Many versions of the same story are told every week, on the same day of the week, and at the same hour of the day. The patient and I, artist/analyst are like a couple holding onto the reins of eight chariots of compulsion. We are racing against three gates of hell. Each session we mend the roads over which compulsions have travelled. For fifty minutes we race the hellions of hell with words and hope to close their gates.

Atonement

According to tradition, on Yom Kippur (Day of Atonement, Repentance) G-d seals the Book of Life and Death for the coming year. At its conclusion, the Gates of Heaven are closed, hence the fervor of our supplications.

"Open the gate for us, at this time when the gate closes, for the day is fading away."
(Artscroll Yom Kippur Machzor (Sefrad version, p. 775).

Unbearable: Braided Bread

Trampling upon the layered and intertwined objects of life
that are less than and not more than
endangered grasses and straw
Marchers, crowd gatherers, and modern day road
runners pound the land and raise fountains of dust
in overused public spaces
Exuding perspiration and dampening a great
thunderous noise
Coal, gas, oil, poison, and sputum all simmer in steel
furnaces and pulsate like harp strings stretched
across the moaning, end of day, empty, muted sky
Mother and her dark matter are contracting.
Mother, dark matter, contracting.
Misunderstood outcasts in attics and gated
communities reek of centuries old misconceptions,
mismatched, misheard, and misspoken, and not-
like-me are kept behind closed doors
Puppet-like prophets, magicians, sibyls, seers, and
talking heads occupy cobwebbed minds and
resurrect what is best left buried in the slippery,
umber-tinged mud of vaulted tombs
The broken and unbearable among us once swelled
with sacks of great breath and heard buglers herald
the call for Mothers baking early morning,
braided bread.

(in memory of my mothers)

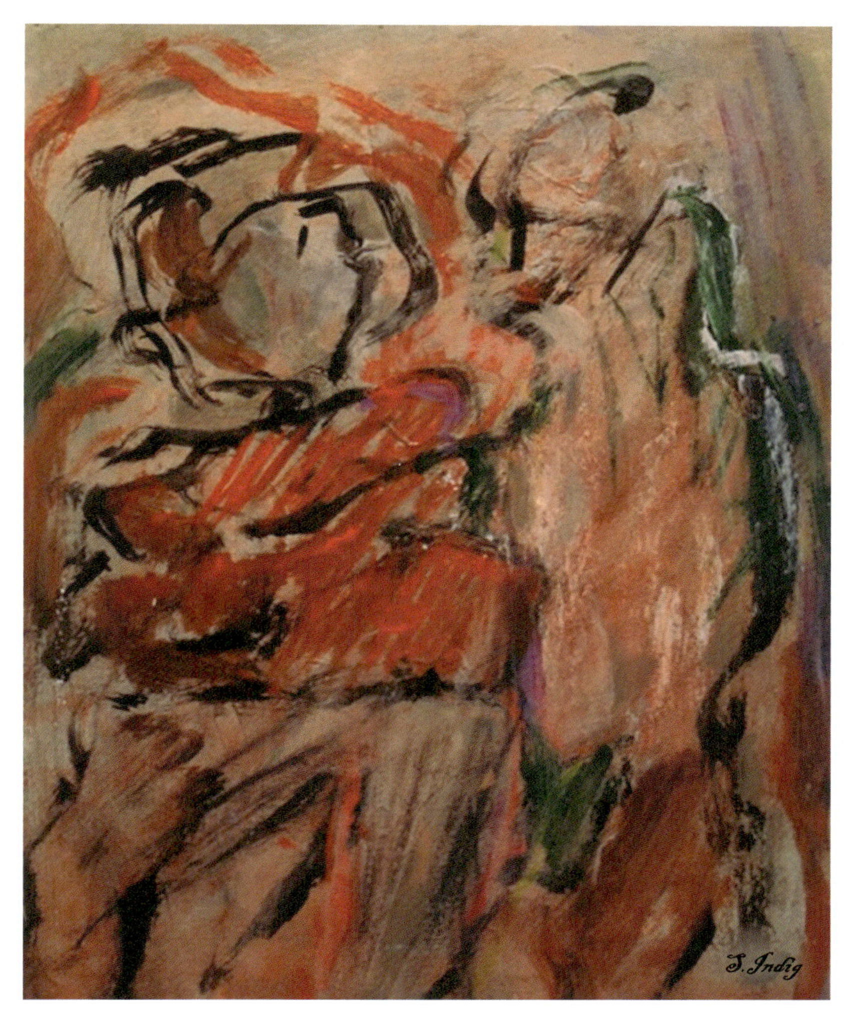

Unbearable: Braided Bread

A Darker Side of Gray

I cannot face you if you don't seek my eyes.
Toothless omens, shattered shards of crockery, fired clay sinks into mingled waters,
The artificial blue with the not quite white join without contraction . . . or exhalation
rhythms of familiar cadences silence sound carried by labored breath.

Crunching the roar and drone of fossil fueled engines,
Four-way traffic of persons displaced in their own land; travelers
of the tar-topped road and burning gravel.

Withered spirits shrink dreams and bend backs.
Permeable silhouettes,
faceless warriors carry black gold
revealing the darker side of gray.

Comment on divisiveness,
division for gain,
and dirty dealings centuries old,
address the question,
"How much is enough?"

(tribute to Simon Wiesenthal)

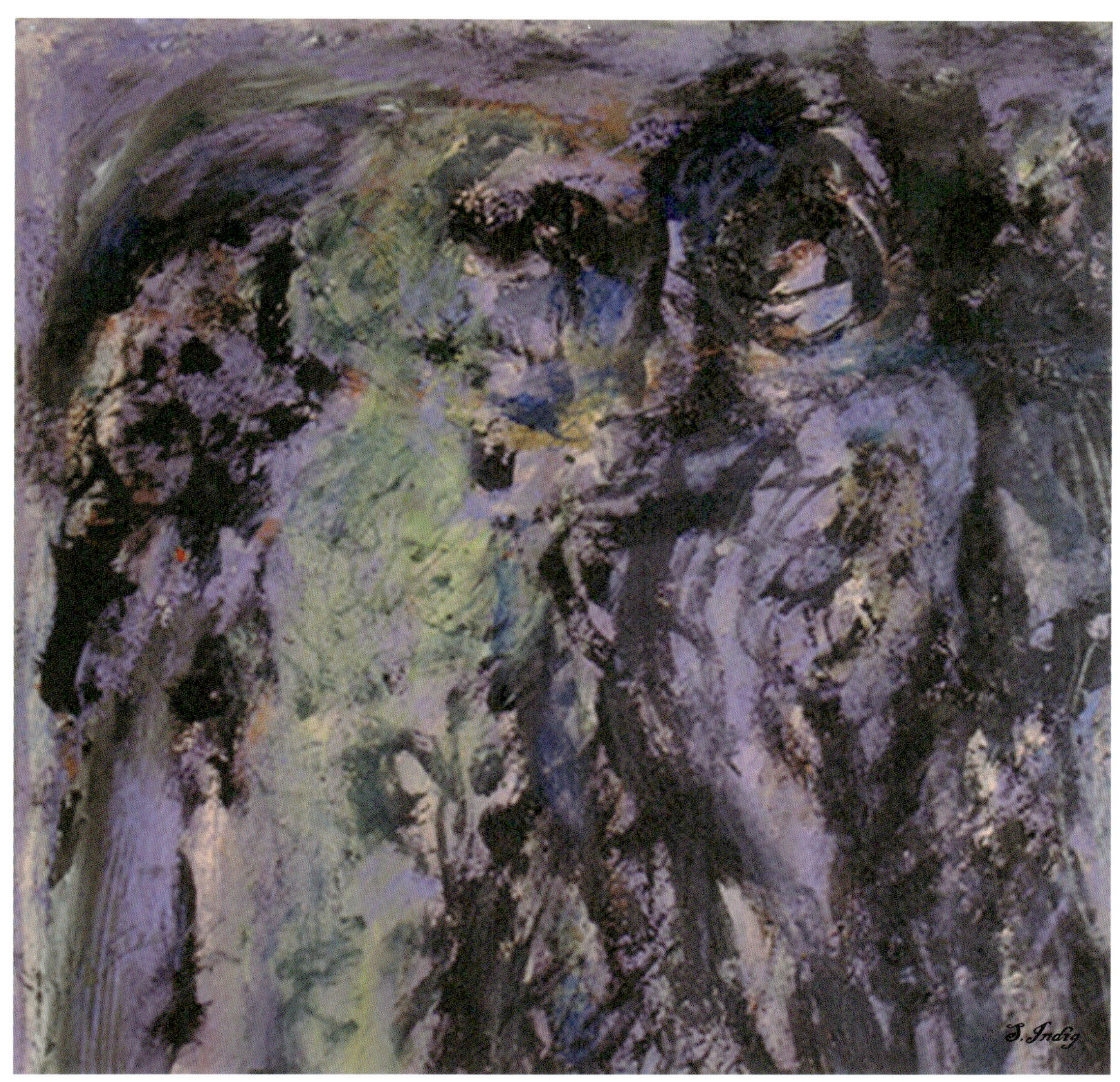

A Darker Side of Gray

Mingled Water (after Hakohen)

From this day on,
teeming waters shall be seen:
jets of water from below
torrents of water from above;
male and female mingled waters;
sweet and salty waters with waters.
And when the clouds
are laden with water,
they shall empty
the male upon the female waters,
to inseminate the waters.
And by them shall they conceive,
give birth and to sprout,
from the heaven of heavens.

". . . and G-d said and let the waters swarm abundantly with moving creatures that have life."
Genesis 1:20

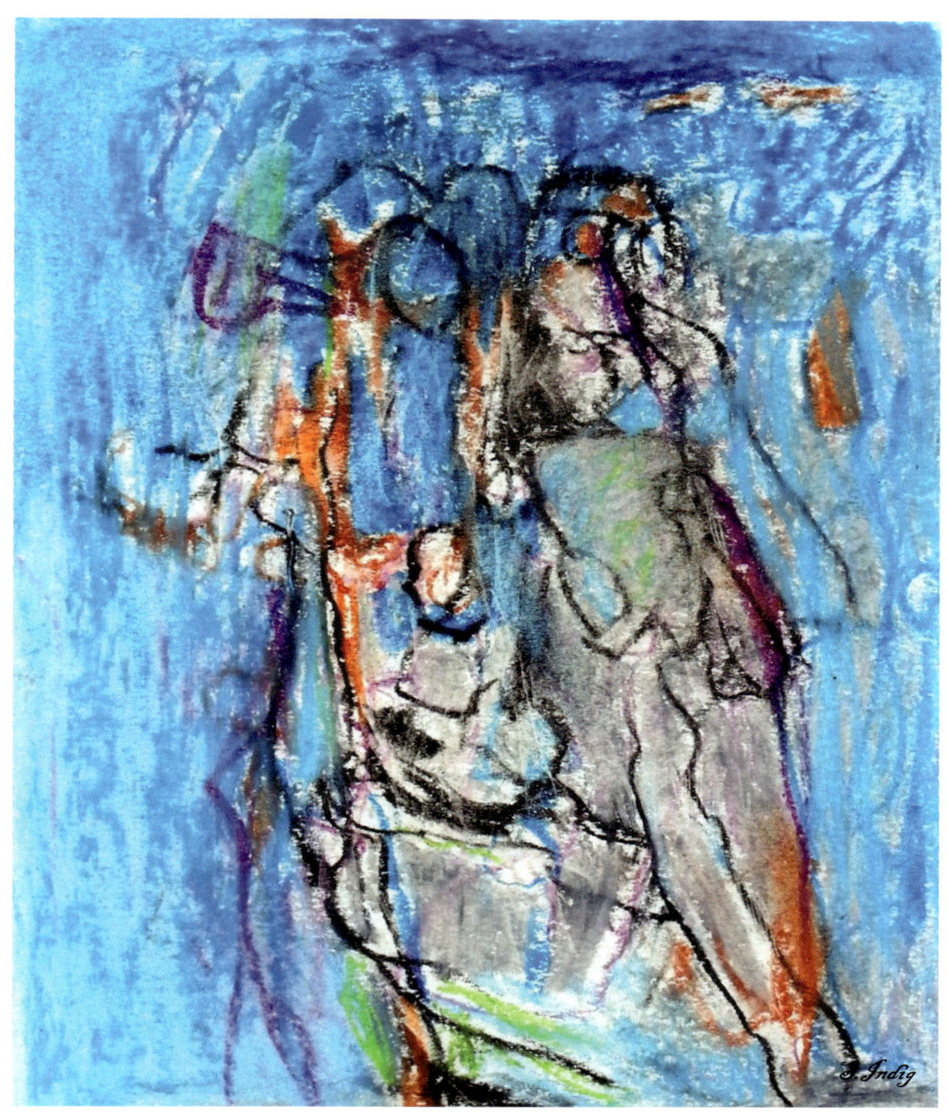

Mingled Water (after Hakohen)

Camp 9: Cancer and Threads of Hope

Costly monuments, weighty memorials, and mind numbing
testimonials addressed to the buried, burned, and beheaded
because they were not like us, not like me;
they were most like the other, the mysterious *them*.
The *they* were akin to lost, dispensable and disposable addresses
supposedly written somewhere on the blank pages of an unbound book.
Images of the imagined were recorded on bronze reliefs
and nailed to red brick walls often illustrating dank cells hidden under dark stairwells.
Both the allegedly innocent and the envious guilty were offered
fragments of unspoken stories recorded on informational plaques
meant to describe the *numbers* found guilty of standing apart,
of failing to comprehend or understand an unknowable
and indecipherable vocabulary. A lack of connection came before an absence of recognition.
There never was an exchange, a lasting treaty or a flimsy truce.
There were traces of memory imprinted on the hands of both takers and receivers.
A majestic monument soaring to the heavens like a mighty eagle is not
always a plea for the clouds to form and cause rain or a prayer for peace.
It is not always a symbol of amends to the living or the dead,
when a simple act of washing hands would have sufficed.

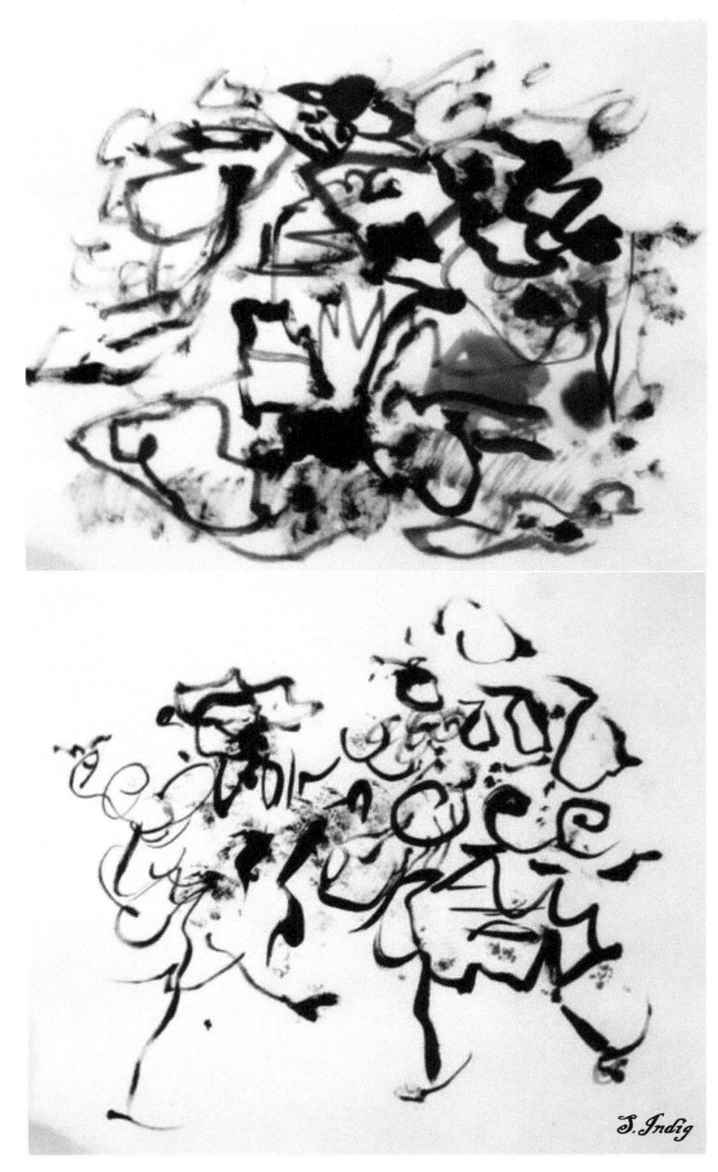

Camp 9: Cancer and Threads of Hope

Red Alert

Stretching into the darkness, covering a sacred incision
Bandaging the soul with an endless in and out,
Back and forth and back again focus . . .

An elusive form in which to pour the detritus of thoughtless thought . . .
The unkind word, the jealous rage, the insatiable greed
Of the too judgmental tenants of a murderous world.

Bomb upon bomb carry the vaporized, heated blood of the red heifer
Cloud of our souls, pale shadows migrating between light and dark . . .
Angels pull veils of the yet unborn away
From voices too loud, teeth too white, and muscles for show.

The question is, "Who tends to the Word
And warms the bread or gathers the tears
To fill the holes of flash floods and screaming sirens?"

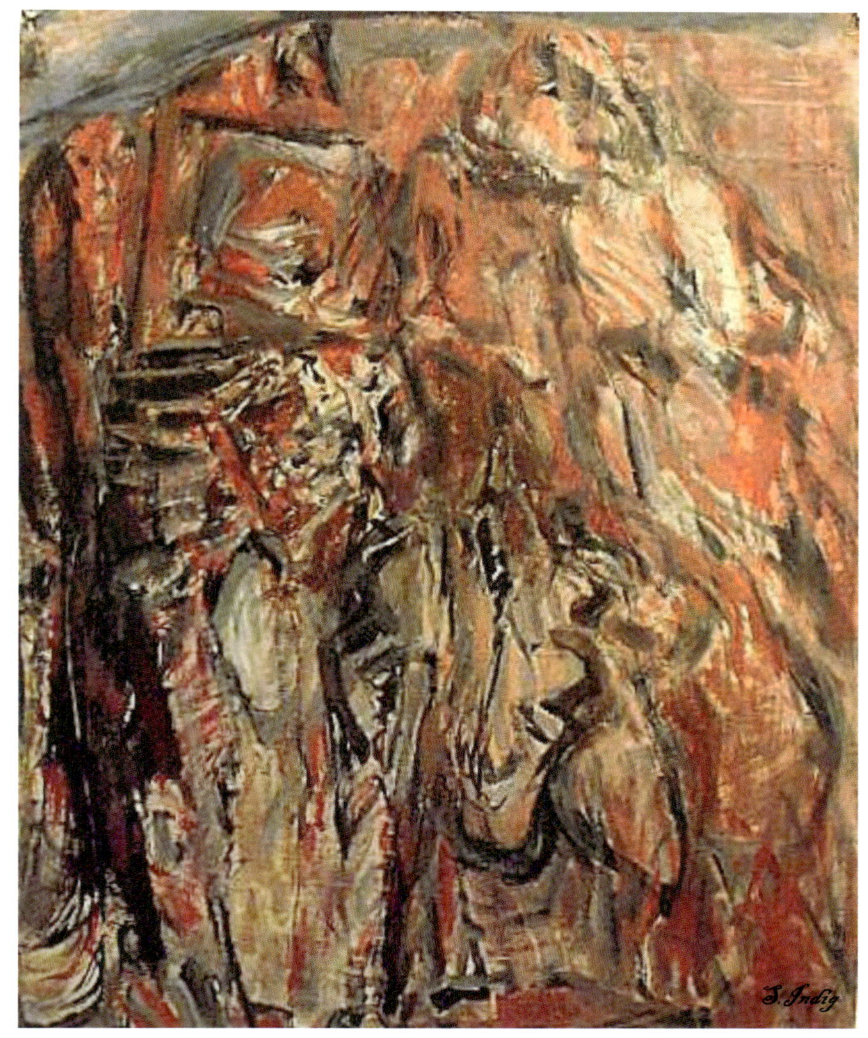

Red Alert

Broken Skin

Once upon the objects of life that are less than and not more
Crowd gatherers and road runners lay down fragile grass
        on pebbled, brown spaces
Exuding perspiration and making a great, thunderous, noise.

Puppets, prophets, magicians, and screeching birds
        occupy foggy minds and choked up souls.

Buried in the slippery umber-tinged mud of cemeteries for outcasts
and attics reeking of misplaced misconceptions, mismatches, misheard,
        misspoken, and misunderstood
            keep the unbearable – behind closed doors and
            Beneath the Broken Skin

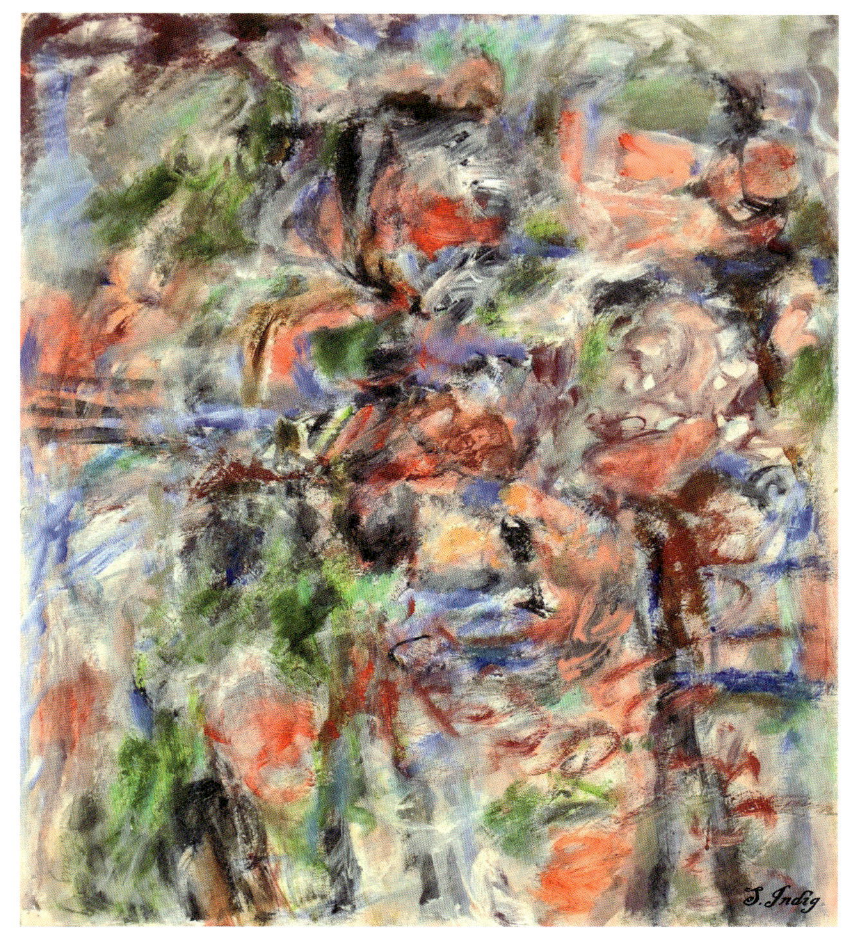

Broken Skin

Time Evaporated

They are not alone inside pockets of warm darkness
Blanketed by a welcomed and prolonged silence
They were once bathed by the great sun of day.

Now they wait outside tents to watch
White walls waiting for brackish brown lithographic ink
To run down their pale, stone faces,
And pool in pockets of imperfection, indentations, and impasses,
Like a spastic cough.
They stop here and there to welcome a sea of clouds
Swimming smoothly into cobalt blue skies covering all
With a veil of evaporated memories.

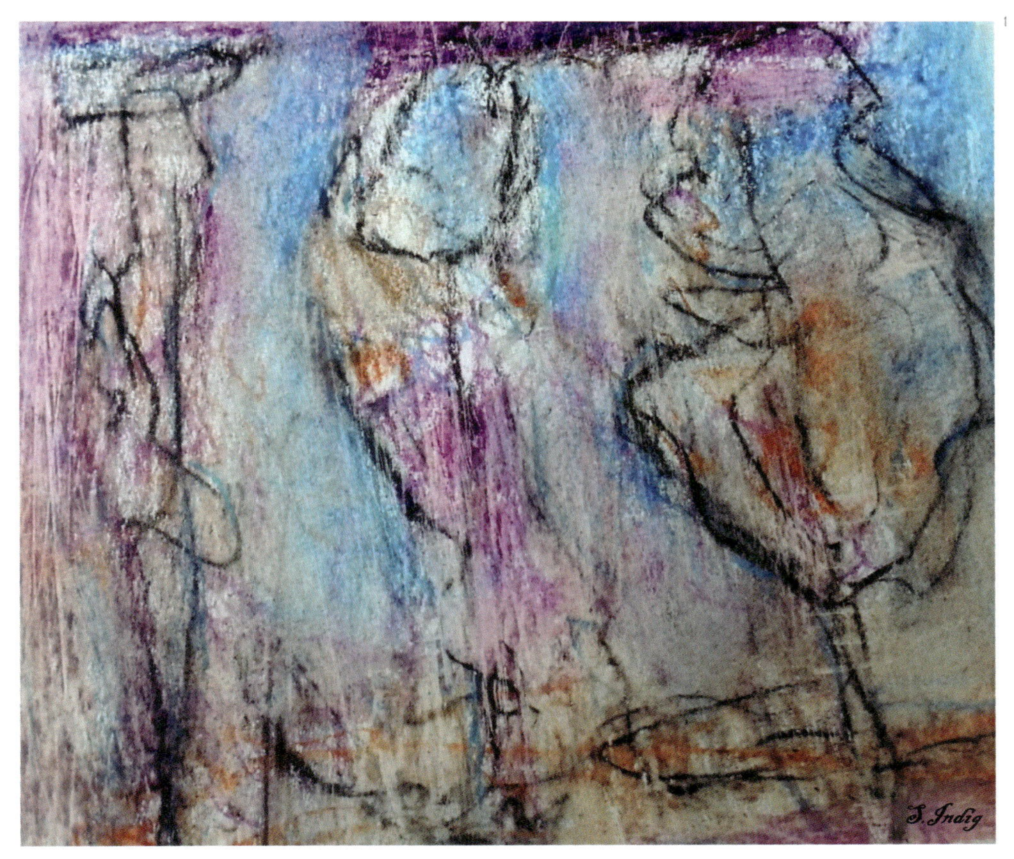

Time Evaporated

Separated

In the beginning
Light was not everywhere at once
nor evenly sown
Who is there to see the great oak fall?
Or hear its far-flung acorns
crack the wall of golden glass,
which once separated Wind from Fire.

"Light is sown for the righteous and for the upright of heart, gladness."
Psalm 97:11

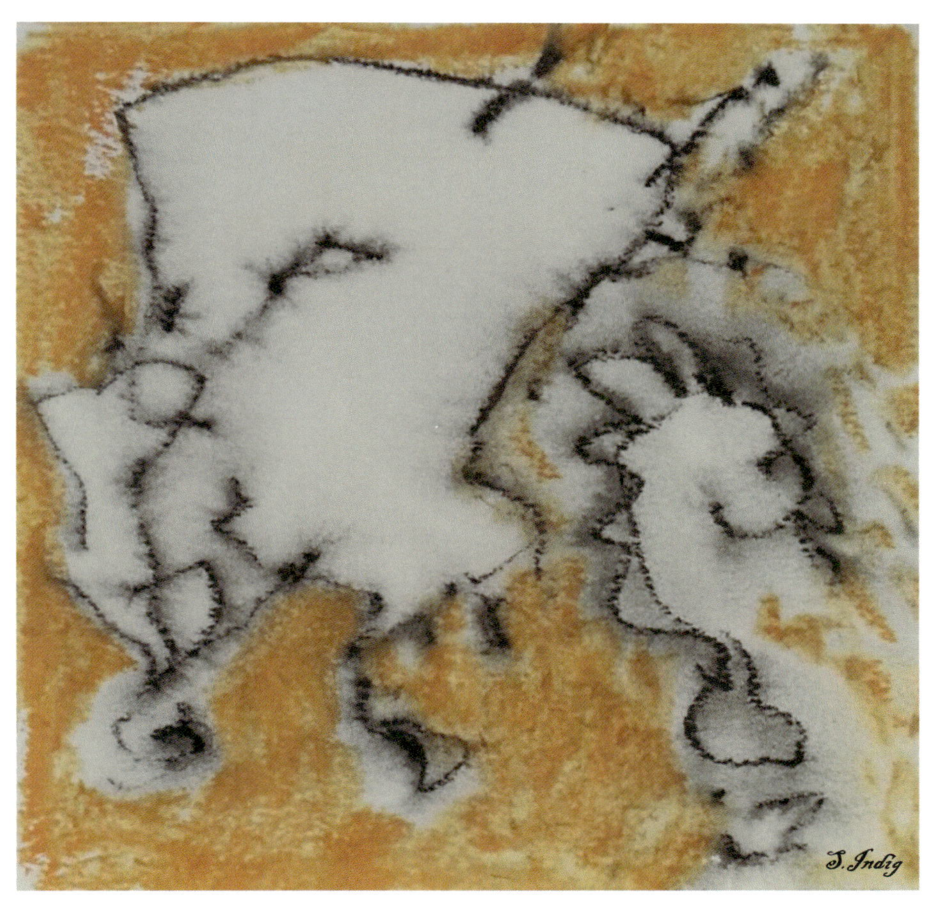

Separated

Wall of Prayer

Stretching into the darkness, covering a
sacred incision
Bandaging the soul with an elusive form
in which to pour the detritus of thoughtless
thoughts and unkind words
Feather upon feather carry the vaporized
heated blood of the red heifer.
Cloud of our souls, pale shadows migrating between light and dark
angels pull veils of lace over the yet unborn
away from voices too loud, teeth too white,
and muscles for show.
Our prayers tend to the Word, warms the
bread, and gathers the tears, to fill the holes of flash floods.
Spaces holding prayers, holding dreams of
every generation—each one building a wall
of dreams, a wall of mingled prayers.

(in honor of all places of prayer)

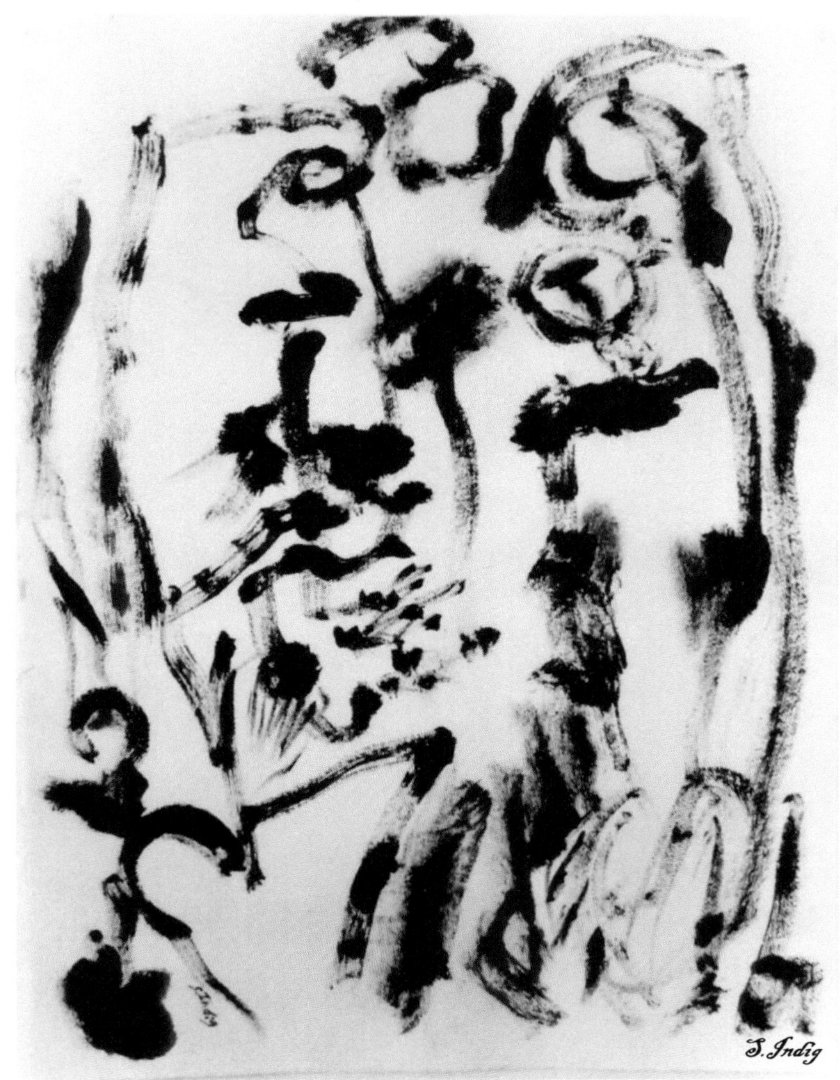

Wall of Prayer

Rolled into Tilson

Rolled out dough
Flattened out dough
Pressed out, slapped down
Eat me when I'm done dough.
       Spilled out, poured on
       Running through a tunnel
       Forced through a pipe
       Turn the tap on.
       Water my blister
           before I burst and swell.
Color of butter mixed in earth
Butterscotch candles, caramel skirts
Raw eggs are better if you add some dirt
          if you add some yellow and a little brown
Birds eat peanut butter when there aren't any worms around.
Rolled out worms
Flattened out worms
       Pressed out and watered down worms.
       Snails in shells roll themselves out
       Double up over
         and come out thin.
Spaghetti in boxes
Caviar in jars
Everything packaged
Leaves us where we are
Pressed out, slapped down, spread out
         peanut butter rolled.

(tribute to Charlie Chaplin)

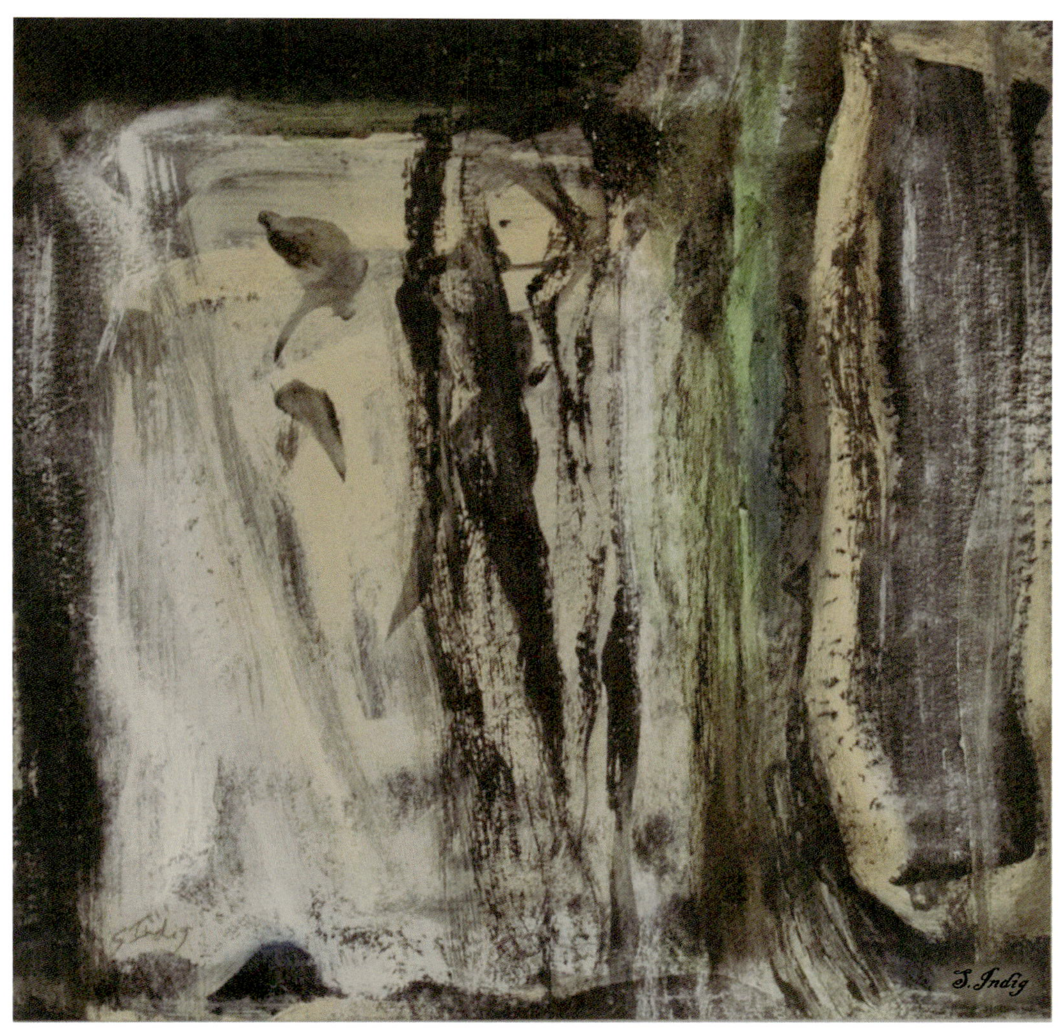

Rolled into Tilson

Listening

that I might crunch the magenta
-like stones a little harder
that I might squeeze droplets of rain
from your layered blonde hair
that I might reach for treasured earthly rewards
and hear the strained struggle of stretched therabands
sliding into hollowed out, after the storm, trees
blue bird songs heard and cups of white tea gulped;
antidotes prescribed for
three million souls and the unfound dead
evaporated before their time
are remembered by the amplified lute
and lit by glistening black coals
burning
when I am not there and they are not here with me,
I stand on their cool blue and white feet
listening.

(tribute to Paul Celan's *Death Fugue*)

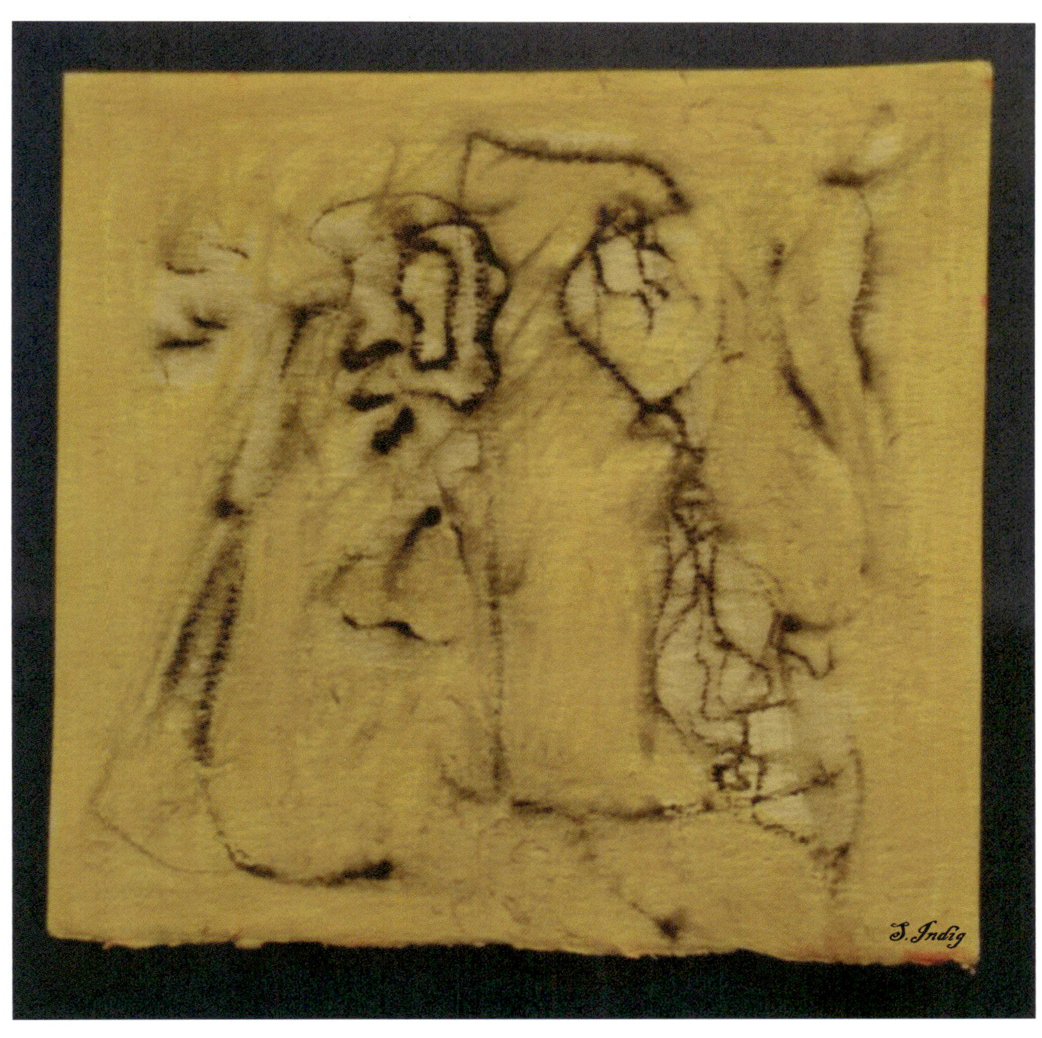

Listening

Repetition in Half–Life

Half-life segments attach memories
together with wreaths
of buttery yellow dandelions
and early vermilion roses
Swept into swirls of inky black water contained by reflected impressions
of old skin creased by searing suns
Memorable and gaping wounds mirror silhouettes of unborn
souls held by punishing ropes of
puppet masters all living in choked up
chimneys sputtering, mumbling
Faulty, careless connections foretell shadows of illusive
flesh-colored walls giving heat to dried bones
Undervalued fantasies,
sculpted-like forms measure
immeasurable time by counting grains of sand,
Losing precious places still celebrated
by iridescent memory-markers
standing end to end
a repetition of half-life segments.

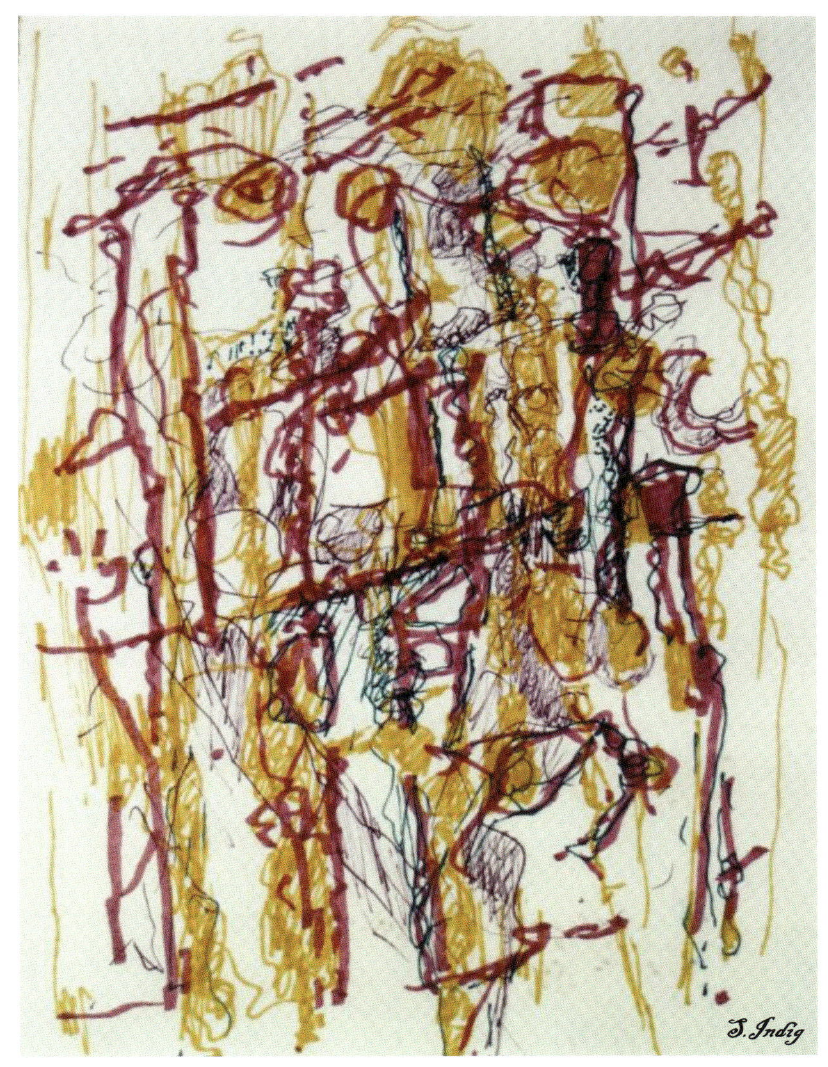

Repetition in Half-Life

Intimate Divisions of Light

Light didn't appear all at once
and it didn't show itself evenly
The middle earth remained in darkness, yet
who first acknowledged cracks
in the heavens and who … heard it last?

How many oaths were whispered and
how many more were expected to be broken?
Two leaves of a wooden book were rubbed
together … many small fires
illuminated saucer-eyed women

They will not see the great oak fall or … hear
tinted acorns shatter the golden glass wall
… the endless wall
which once divided Wind from Fire

Cupped hands fold like the division between day and night
separating the blessed light from their lidded eyes, turning
the gold to red … tinted acorns carry
petitions and meditations
far above the glass wall of their sheltered souls

(Genesis 1:4)

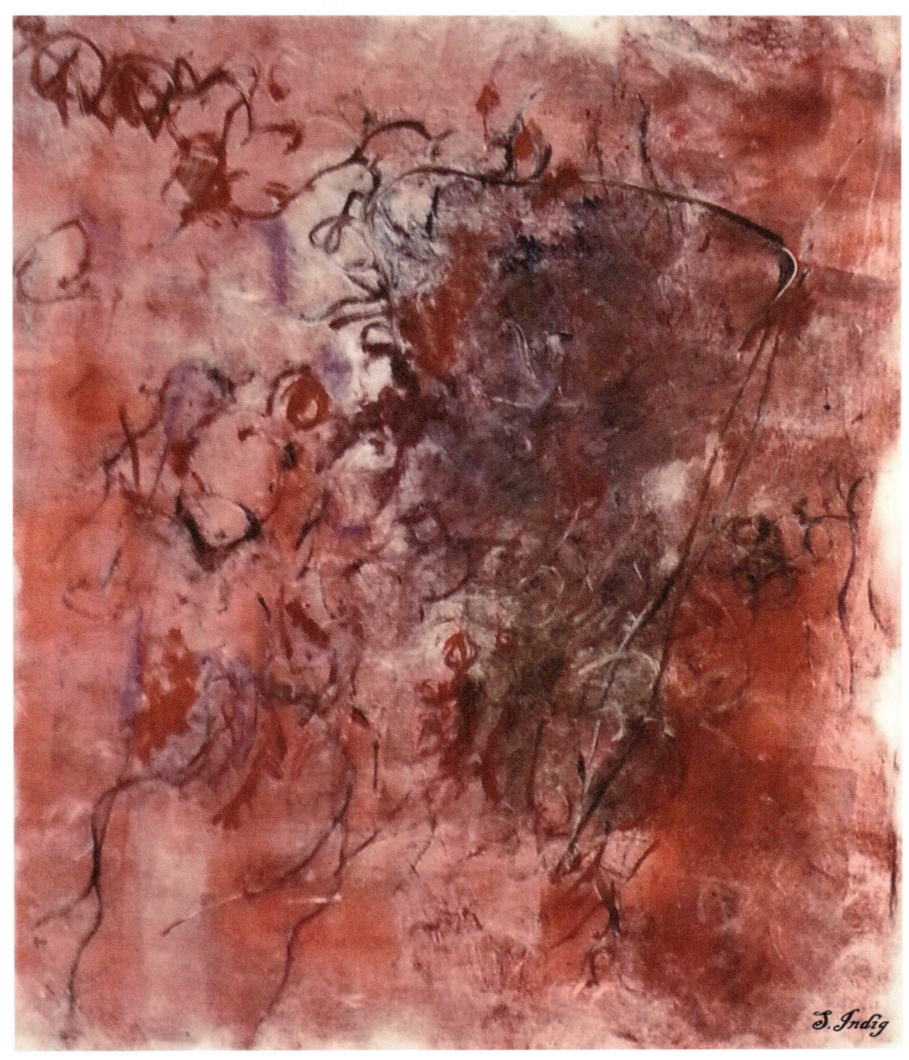

Intimate Divisions of Light

A Small Gift Starting with "C"

Burlap sacks of recorded wisdom

Captured in bubbles of wordless dialogue for the hearing who cannot see and
lullabies for those who cannot speak.

Planks of wood cover cracked sidewalks and
Chewing gum once pink. Smack, Crack, Smack . . .

For the Adagio dancer crisscrosses the hearts
of blue birds soaring under cloud covers

Figurines cut out of paper doilies, the laced boot crowd evaporates on a wind driven carpet

Railroad spikes planted in black earth illuminate the illusion of small gifts starting with "C."

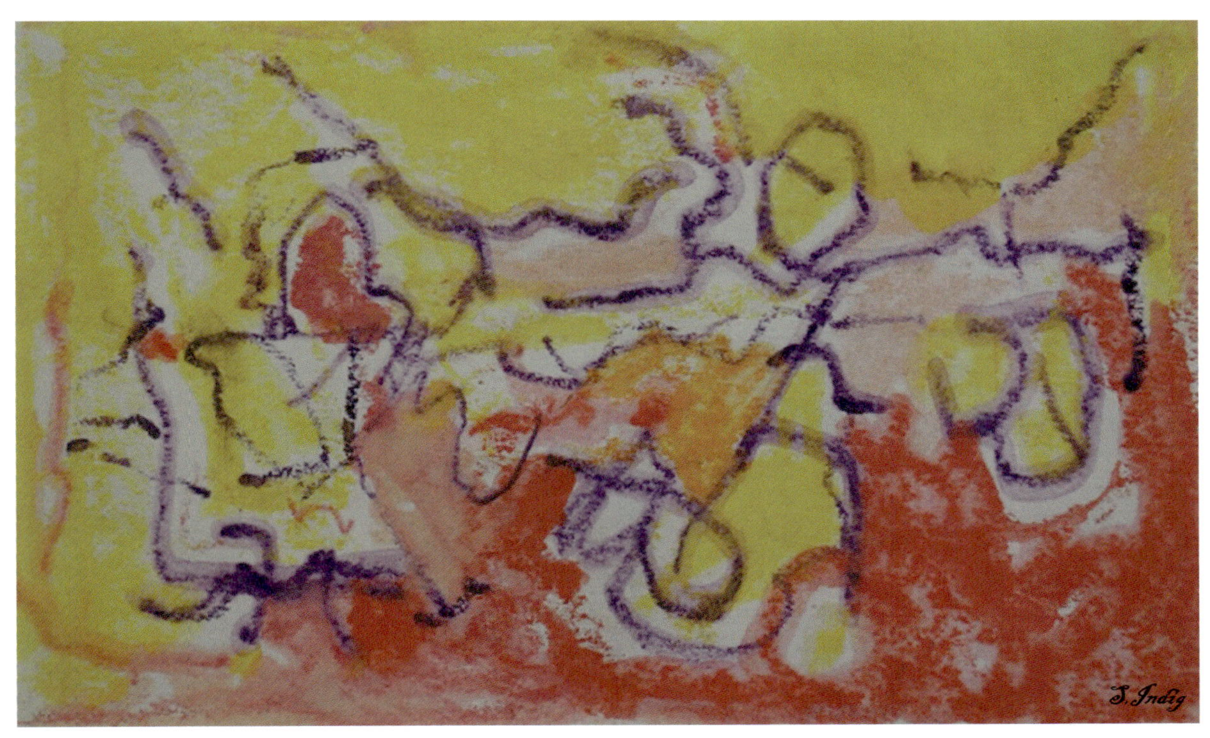

A Small Gift Starting with "C"

Doubling the Life

I am you who speak to me at dawn.
You speak at dawn
And imprint on an impressionable brain
When limbs were too weak to take flight,
Before you breathed me life and held us between two arms
When the world was all color warmed by two look-alike suns
We were then twins; we were twins for one hundred
And twenty years; together we saw through
Stained eyes and mirrored wishes
The life beyond this life, beyond the places of
Fashioned bandanas, tribal colors, and matching moves
Remembering ancient songs that only partners sang;
Sung before the bubbling waters flowed and lifted
Scales from veiled eyes
And loosened feathers from between foreign toes
Placed too far apart; rocking the newly doubled, doubling life.

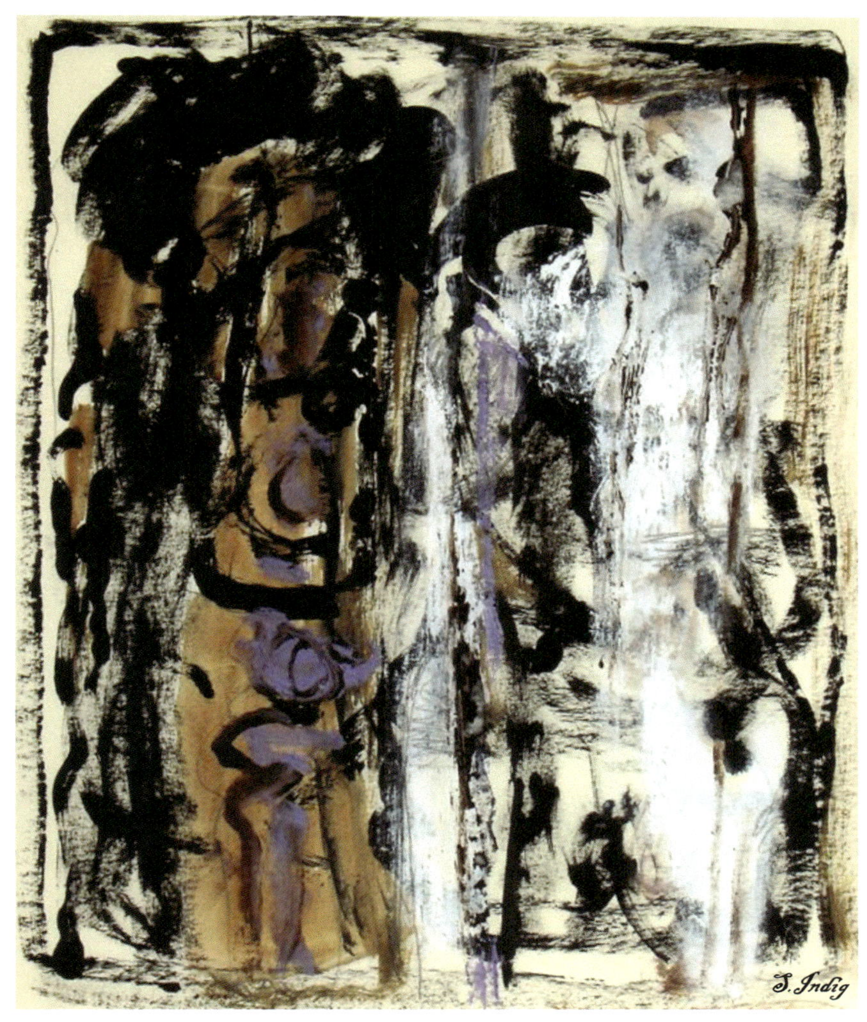

Doubling the Life

A Studied Lady

Remnants of rooms without enough space for the running.
An eyeless sun toasts the Easter eggs black on the ledges
     of painted windows,
Here reason is bought with electric light bulbs,
     Lining rooms with false twilight.

Sadness caresses the locked doors.
She beats her sister fear, daughter of madness
Bringing tears to a body in perpetual sleep.

In the spaces between waking she visits like the wind,
     Inviting birds of song with her toothy duck smile,
     and knowing why silence bangs on like
     damp bed clothing.

Sadness freezes the bridge of wakefulness,
     and bears me welcome in her joyless house.
The remnants of dead rooms, a two dimensional nightmare.

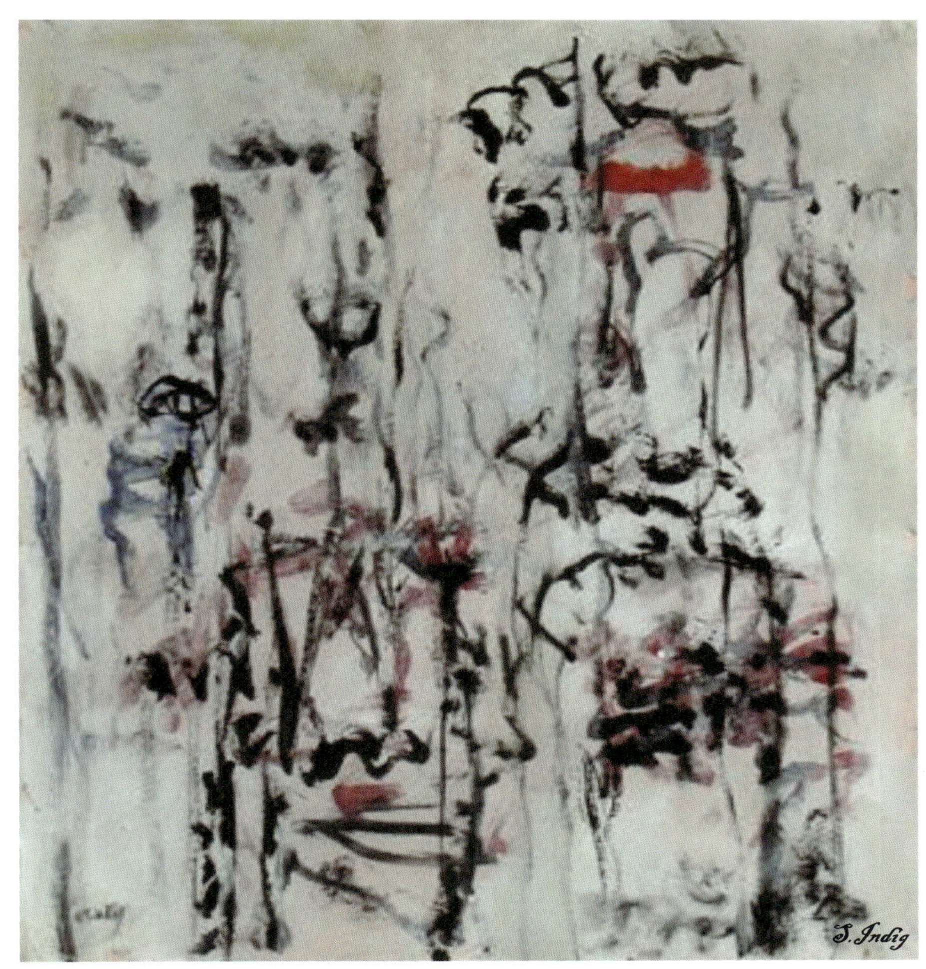

A Studied Lady

In the Studio

Fast smiling dogs travel on wet places breathing out mist with
tongues moving fast to sculpt cracked pink words and crease
the wonder in calm amber eyes.

They water the hot places to lay down blood
on cold stones doing time in crypts.
And the laughter of cows pressed down
The ears of Mary's dog where Very Blue had cradled her
and made confetti of each
letter of each word cut from the New York Times.
Critics called it floor paintings and fried his spine on spigots come
hot of damp places where only the prickly pink flowers grew.
She sees him to hear with the ears of the sleeping dog.

Time licked the mountains clean where panels of light dropped
behind irises closed to an air conditioned sky.
He heard the great cow laugh in her belly breathing *Rock It Very Blue*.
and created the wonder in Mary's calm amber eyes.

(to all past lovers)

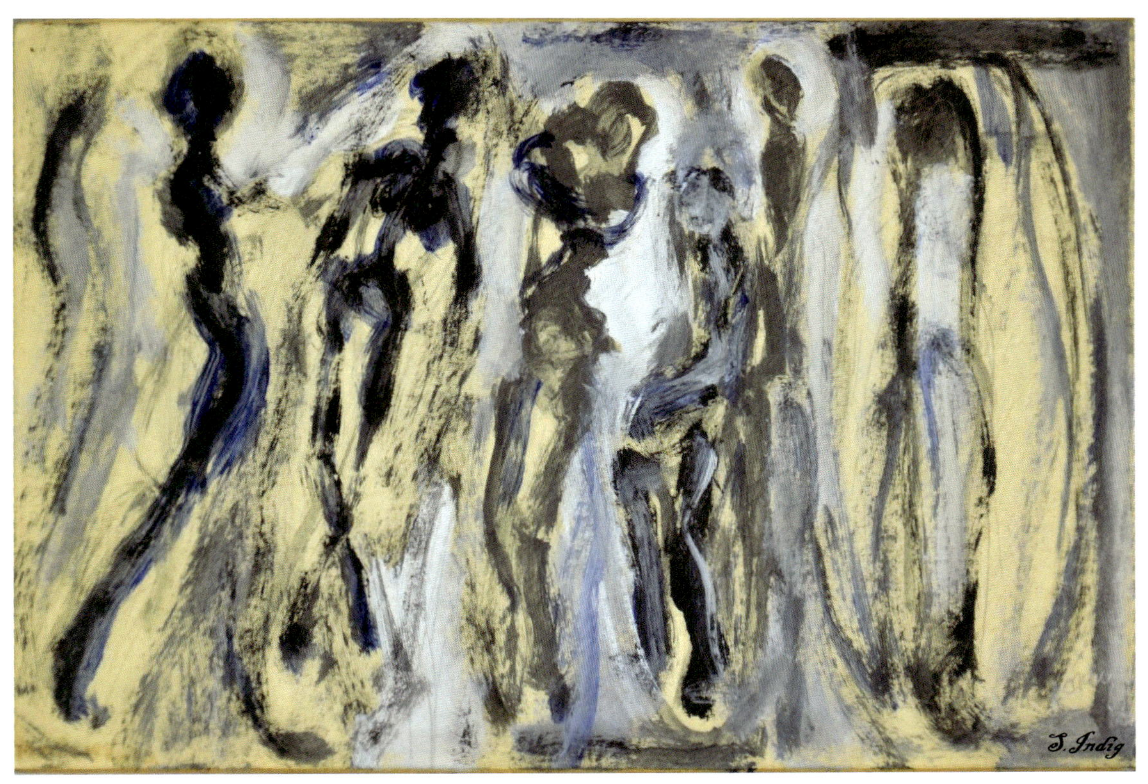

In the Studio

Reflections in Black Plastic

Image — Towers placed where none can breathe.
Heat steams inside rooms sculpting forms
in unwanted places.
      Space — Travel with the wind to blow on tall, friendly
      sandstone statues watching a muddied Atlantic sea.
      Clay shores once reddened with blood. History.
Erasures — Distress is not the fog, the hidden sun,
the drunken laugh heard from darkened sidewalks of
any city drifting with
shadows of small children and orange cats.
Walk on wooden steps and watch wet laundry stand vigil.
      Up and down unbannistered passages.
      Loose threads free of looms and loving hands.
      Predictability drop gobs of metallic paint.
      The snows have yet to come.
Passages — Some lost sight of the railing which once
guided them to the sea.
Despair, unhinged, lacquers already hardened floors.
Small, round flattened stones.
State of Rivere du Loup, a magical place,
an embedded and distant memory.
      Blue carpeted hallways whisper in and out of dreams.
      A magician brought the coast road
      and its charcoal grey Ryder's moon.
      Whirling zinc clouds sweeping black water clean.
Image — Eyes are filled with a lantern-red sun.
At the day's end, the fifth sun
paints broad stripes of grass.
Shadows of trees still giving reflections
on black plastic.

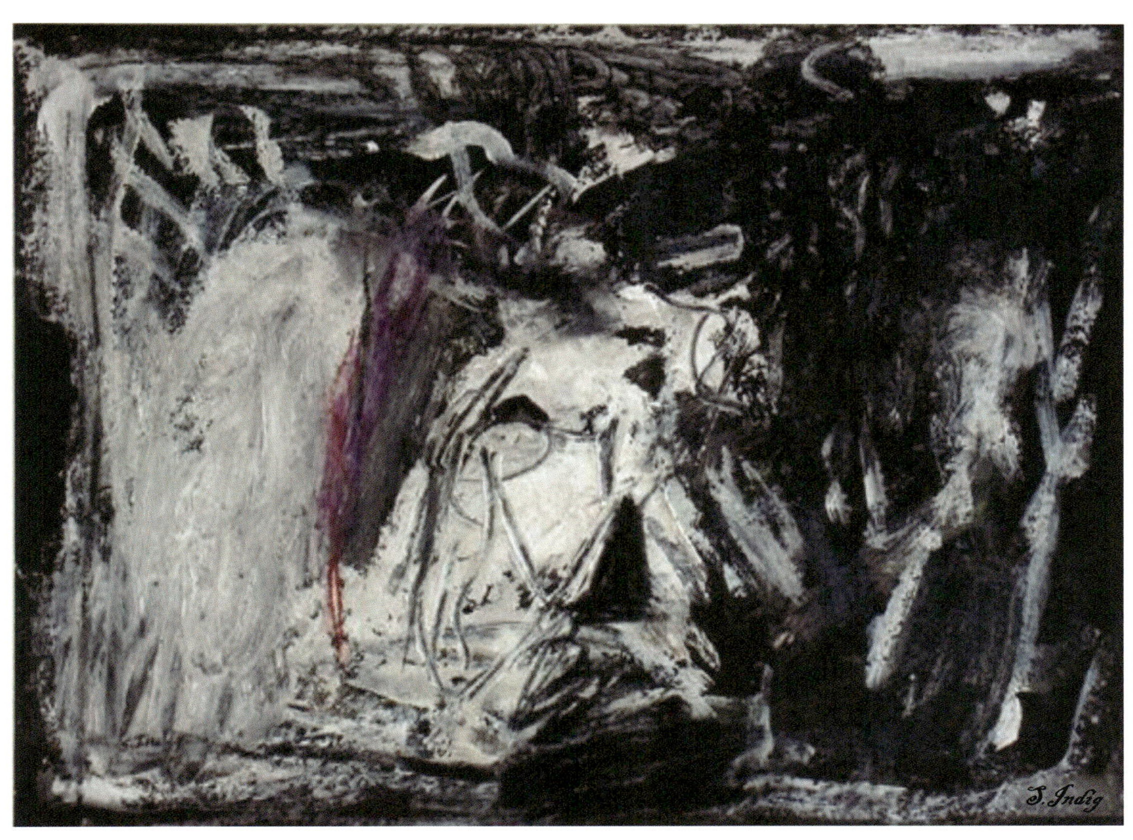

Reflections in Black Plastic

Shelter

Dark markings etch into
the great white void announcing
Shabbot's sheltering angels of
golden lights turned red between
two cupped hands bearing souls
across the river between us.

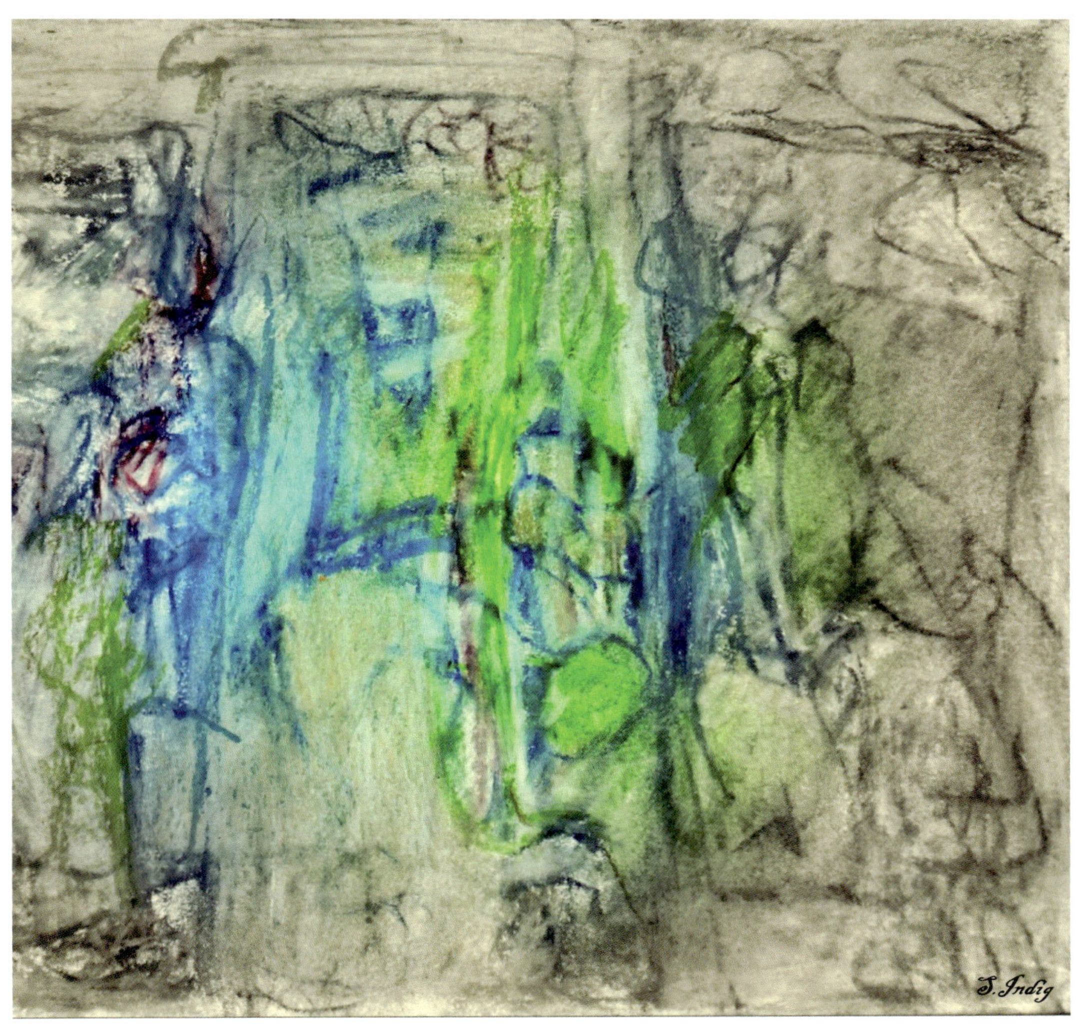

Shelter

Unspoken

And you are remembered to me.
You who walk on the edge of all cloud-light
Between two lines where I breathe and
       drink in the blue of sin.
Layers of the warm, of the warmest fluid
Darken the edges of Queen Anne's lace.
You dance to an orgy of gurgling black milk, framed
      by a mirror singing into the
      tunnels of my ears.

A silent dust contracts in the midst of ripened flowers
      roasting me in the folds of my silken sails.
The Indian dancer always remembers.

In her splashing breath she runs to a place where the candle
      shadows read to her the story of living as she was in
      private unused spaces.
And I love you walking on the edge of all cloud-light.

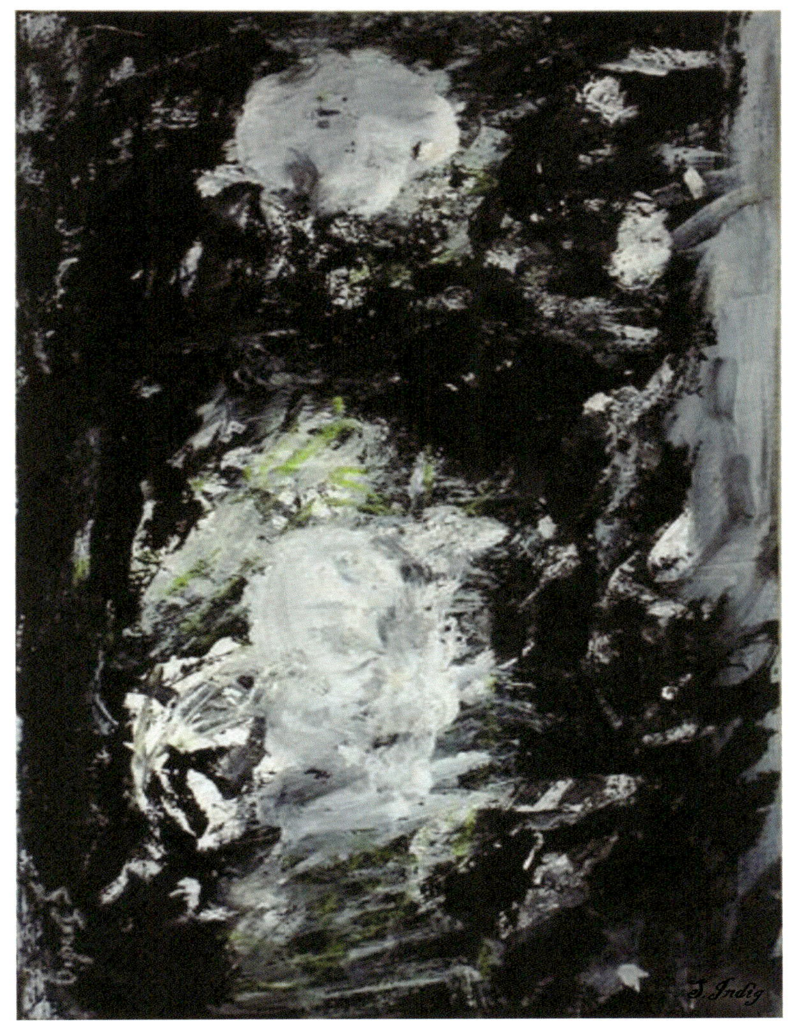

Unspoken

Ruffina's Bliss

Your memory presents in the fine weave of old lace;
            patience, endurance, and love.

Your memory fires: green apples, stained glass, and
            majestic windows
all adorning glistening hallways that are without repetition.

They will not to be crossed again or will they fade away
from lack of footsteps stopping at the sculpted doorways
            of many colored light.

Jewels born of vision detain the riotous ones' straining to
breathe, while longing to tremble with the chimes of
            colliding glass.

A cobbled together dream raids the resting mind
shattering all that was visible through white laced curtains.
Separating what is knowable from what
            I have come to call, "me."

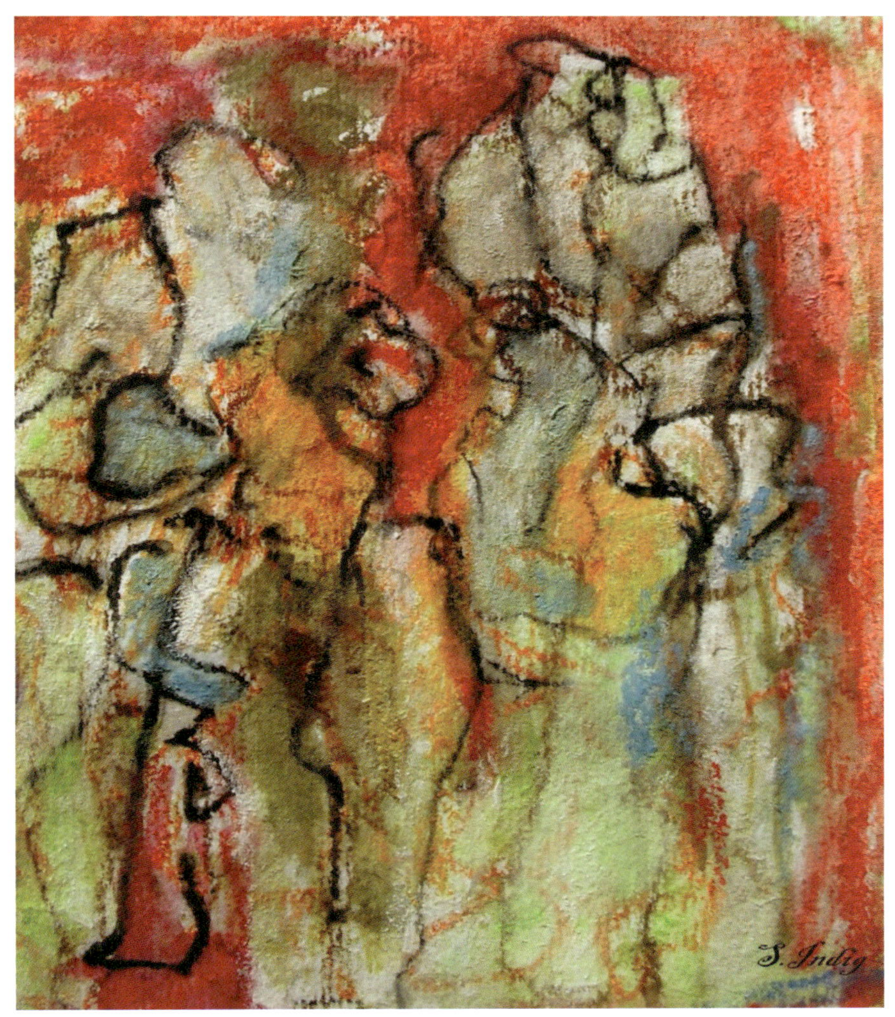

Ruffina's Bliss

Pale-Green

She rises before us not as herself but obscured
       by a vast pale-green veil.
In what direction does the edifice that Catherine built face?
In her northernmost sky, vernal vision gives solace to the weary,
       the weakened, and the sick of heart,
Her grand courtyard, now a sea of both slushy and hardened ice,
       calls the less-than to merge their flickering flame with her mighty one.
Torrential rains and eternal snows tighten her already firm
       grip until the miracle of her white nights fills her great belly.
Her food smells of small fears and desires both wonderful and dreadful.
The greenness of her sky paints itself on the palace of winter.
Ivan IV (the Terrible) surrounded by his Black Guard, the *oprichniki* and
King David's shield of love and poetry, heaven on earth, both guard the
       House of Catherine, the repository of mankind's jewels from
       those unable to create; from those who rage and destroy.
In the liminal light of visions, the warrior and dreamer are one,
       the beholder of truth and beauty, both pure and impure.
She is flexible and elastic, a shape-changer and sometimes a green line, and
       sometimes just as she is: the dancer, poet, scribe of our stories.

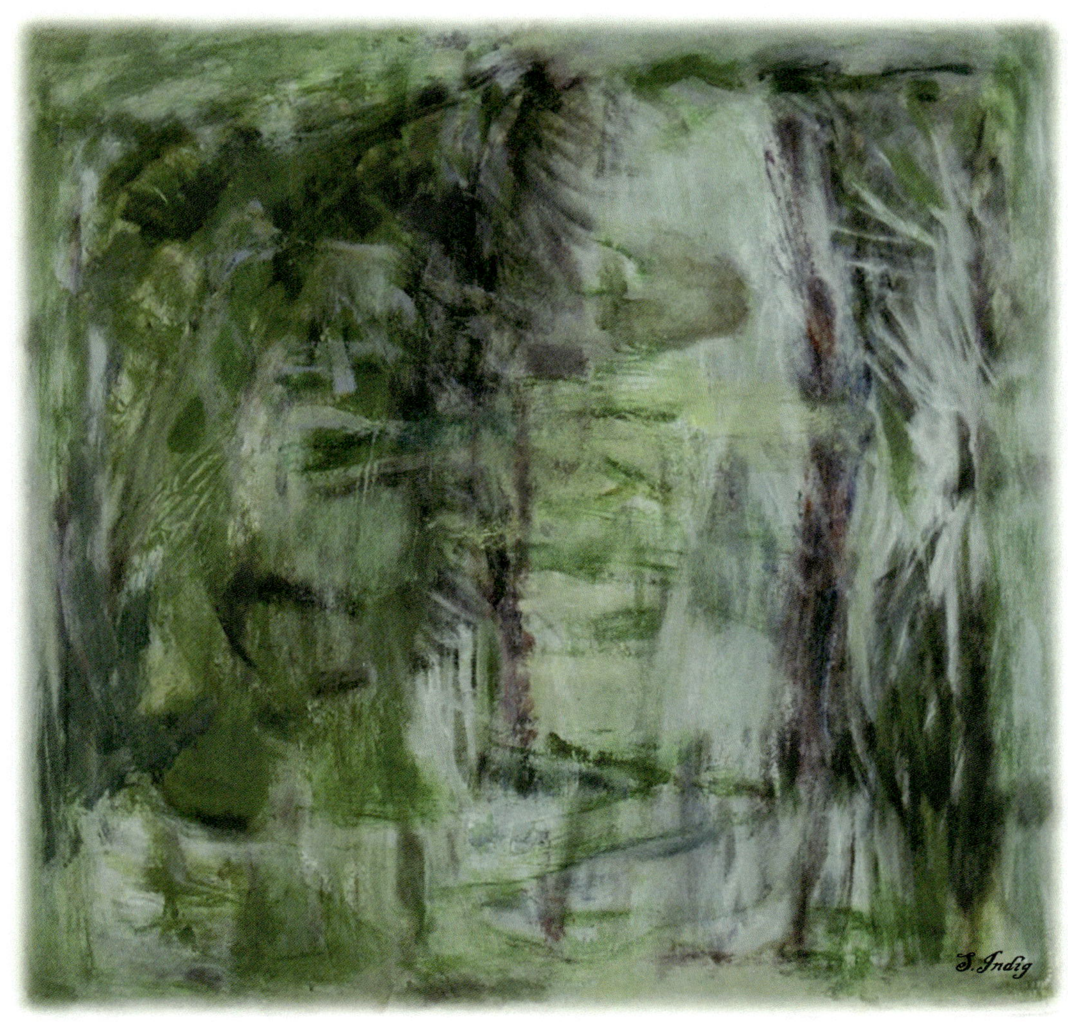

Pale-Green

47

Guests of the Sleeping Mind

You become known to me when you lean against the doorposts of my rooms.
You are known to me when you enter and then again when you leave
touching doorposts with warmer hands. Your many faces remain over time,
in the life-time of seasons, in the shadows of oak trees lit by many suns.
The light rests against pillows of shifting clouds rarely perforated by rain drops and pushed
by dancers riding the waves of wind. You are in the oceans of words,
in the shapes of changing thoughts. You sail in the ships of youth and in the swimming tides
of the long lived.

You walk in dreams folded into images of collapsed and condensed time and
talk through hieroglyphics. You see in pictures burned into colored balloons of thought.
You light the fires in the bellies of the graceful movers creating poetry
in space and moving between and through the density of waking hours.

In your anger, your fear pricks the torn air that pulls mountains apart and divides the seas.
You drift within a shattered heart and wallow in the marrow of broken hope lain on piles of
bones waiting to be born again. In your multiplicity you are the One who weaves into the
warp of golden thread ribbons of red, of blue, and of purple. A cloth destined to dress
souls honoring celebrated seasons.

Your tapestry is the shroud dried on winter's body. The tapestry is the color in spring's
blush, the curve in summer's smile, in the pigment of fall's rainbow colored leaves and
fading flowers. In days of mourning your dreams are whispered by the eternally
remembered.

She was carried into the days of mourning. She was lifted by the arms of
her seed and guided by the night vision of the ancient ones. The weavers of our days are
known by eyes seeing between light and dark. They lifted their eyes into a time when there
was no time but only the warm hands of guests
touching doorways of sleeping minds.

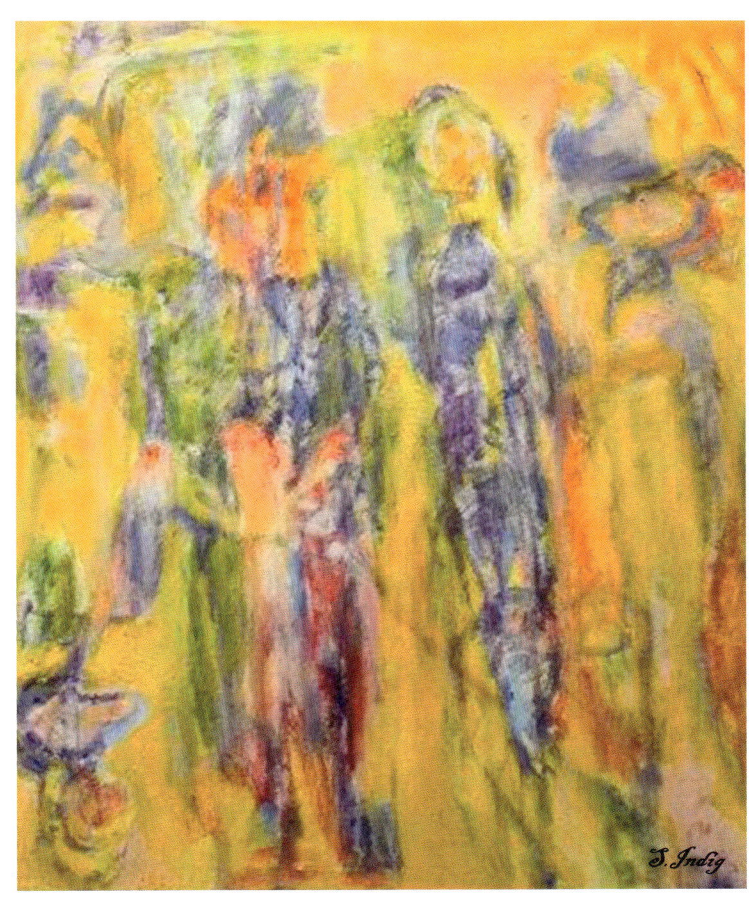

Guests of the Sleeping Mind
(Triptych, panel 3 of 3)

Silence the Dimmed Light

She came upon the resting night shadows
whispering vows
Given on forty journeys
over eighty-four years
A great seduction of accumulated
promises made in unfamiliar lands
hills and rivulets
run through man-made
negotiated boundaries
where air hangs heavy
under unforgiving suns waiting for a path.
Lights search but only find dark clouds
A sudden sneeze is muffled in a shirt-sleeve, as
gnats swarm, circling rotating heads
like crusaders' swords.
Her silent scream could shatter eardrums,
while hordes of silent worms strain to vivify
Parches of reddened soil.

(tribute to Leonard Cohen)

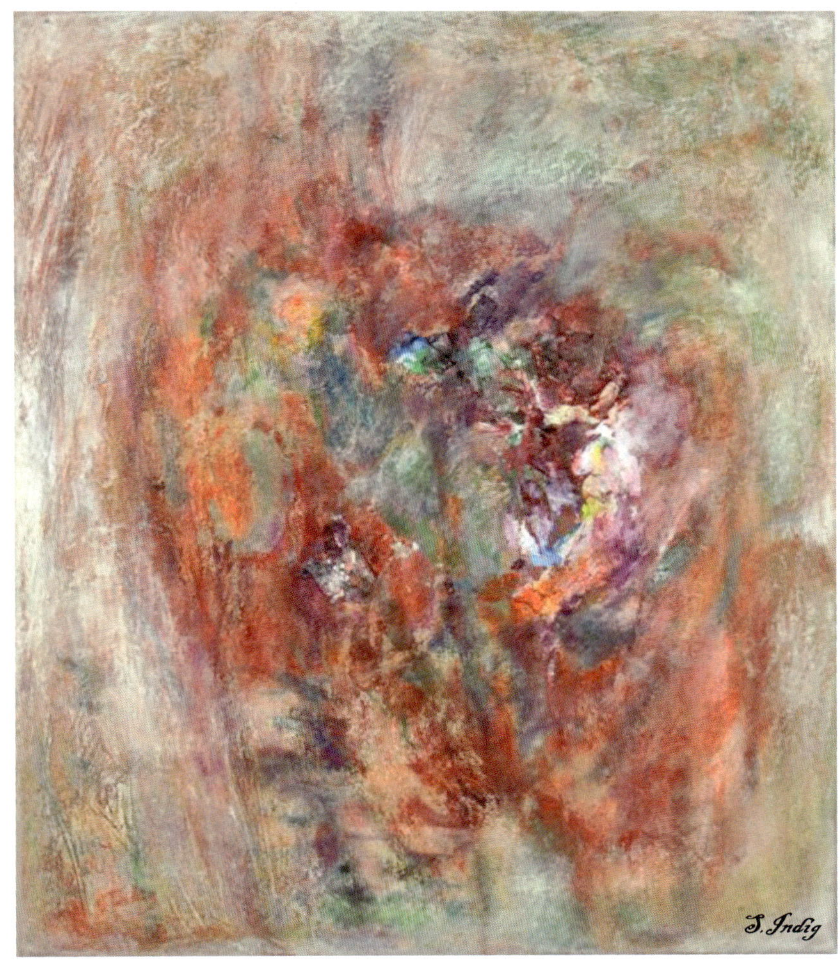

Silence the Dimmed Light

The Invisible One

The Invisible One
is enclosed in colored glass;
A room of rose colored glass without a door,
No door that earthly eyes can see,
An opened heart can find a way in and through
Without shattering,
Without noise;
A carpet of desire is laid between us
Shrinking distance and decades
A grand hug locks in all light;
The opened glass door holds the red
jewel of life
and the circumcised heart.

"Who is like you, Master of mighty deeds, and who is comparable to you…"
Shemoneh Esrei – Amidah

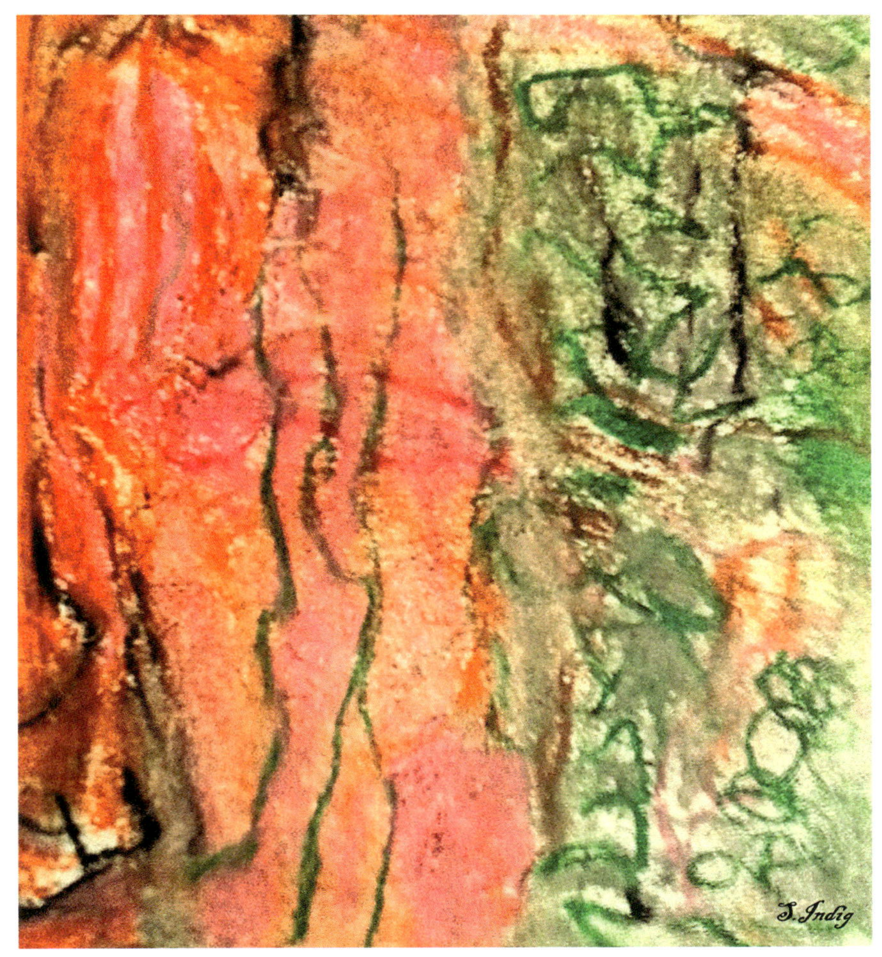

The Invisible One

After–Image Collected

And you can't get it together after the river bed
          has been filled to a rising stoned-together sienna,
Muddy water running with cans of Rheingold and blue
          Coca-Cola
You didn't see the chicory cornflowers because Miss
          Rheingold is billed on Interstate 95
Covered by piped music—perforated exhaust fumes
          that didn't give in time what it took away,
Like so much stitchery on blue denim, prefabricated
Blown blue dots, shattered flash bulbs and
The lady drops linen handkerchiefs like sign-posts
          along the highway.
Freeze your appetite on substitutes
          The public for free-rolling on blackened wheels
Weaving daisy chains to the tune of "American Pie,"
After the end was one letter, "Z"
The subway cars are steel on graffiti.
An exhibition of frustrated presidential hopefuls.
          some people are always there,
ExxonMobil has visited Philadelphia.

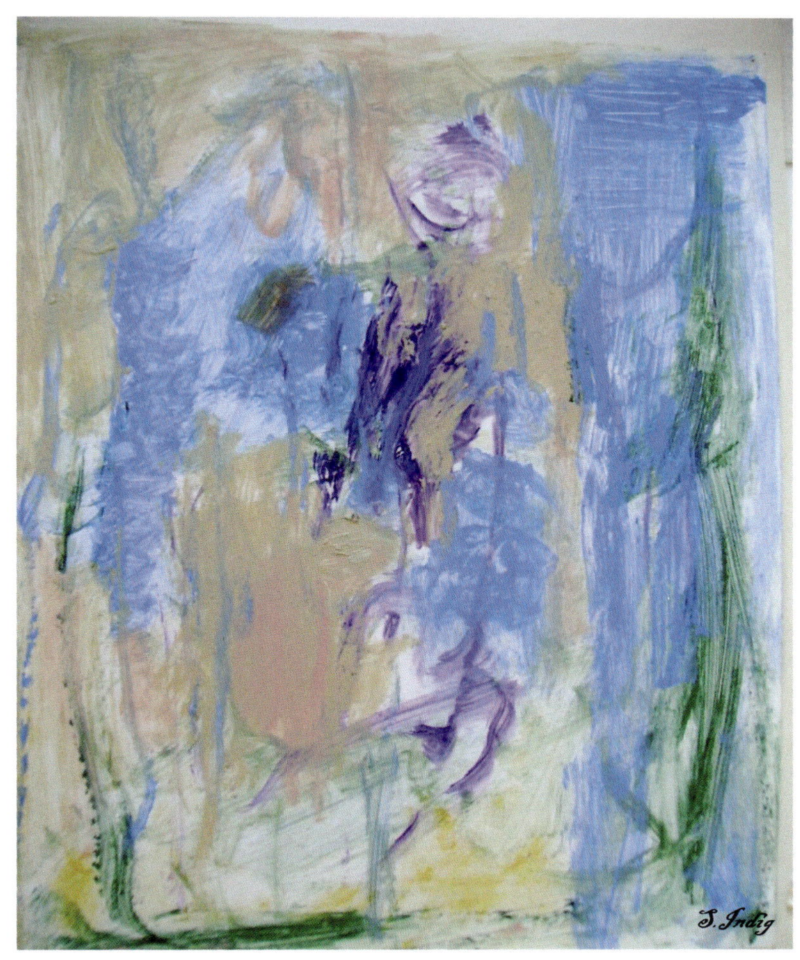

After-Image Collected

Story in the Sky: Remembering 12 Sons

Stories in the sky reverberate behind closed eyes
       safely burrowed inside the folds of time,
       pushing to unravel the resistant night,
       then pausing to rest with waiting, unnamed stars.
Who was born to envision their effervescent colored form
       or to see into the before history of recorded time?
The ancient ones settled into the earth's precious crown
       like so many jeweled memories;
       memories planted in the blood of generations.
Twelve quietly gave themselves up to the deep cave of the darkened
       blue sky, effortlessly partnering with circles of colored light
       emanating from behind the cloak of day.

Older eyes and still older ears hear the story of twelve and
       remember.

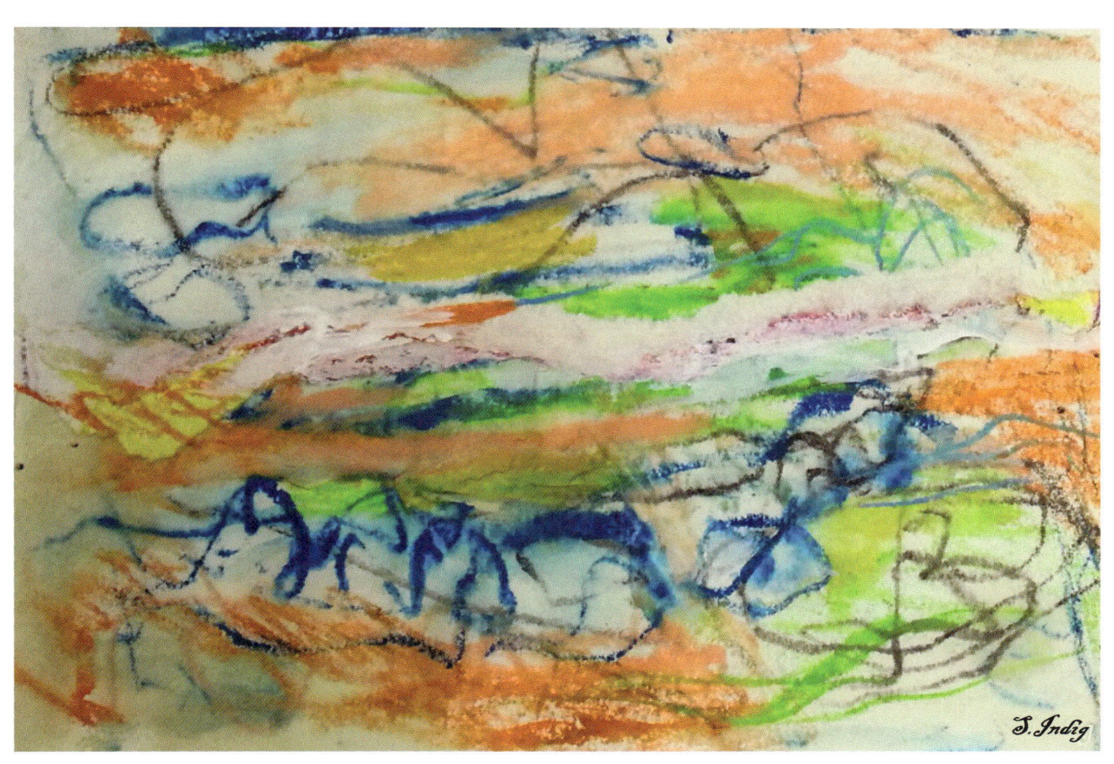

Story in the Sky: Remembering 12 Sons

Acknowledgements

"There is a mountain. On the mountain there is a stone. From this stone, flows a Spring." (Zohar 2:24)

My creativity has many sources that continually refresh it. I count among those sources my close friends and others known to me only through their works.

Dr. Inna Rozentsvit – for her kind and generous support, enthusiasm, and encouragement. Her appreciation of art and science as a symbiosis was the essential force propelling the idea of a book which married several senses into one reality.

Dr. Eva D. Papiasvili – for her appreciation of my poetry and art, and their influence on my clinical psychoanalytic work.

Herman Lowenhar – for the depth of his scholarship, spirituality, and kindness that steadied me when I waivered in the commitment I had made to my creative purpose.

Candace Frede – for lending to me her highly honed grasp of both image and word, articulate use of language, and discriminating eye to the text editing.

Michael Amunategui – for identification of the story-flow, as well as the flow of the images and words into a sequence, creating a seamless, aesthetic whole.

Jackie Shabot – for her honest and straight from the hip responses to the very early version of my work, which was immensely helpful. She is an intuitive critic.

Jiro Naito – for his provocative and profound questions about the book's meaning and intention.

Lawrence G. Smith – for his unwavering support through the many years of creating this book's material.

Dr. Joseph Ament and Mrs. Naomi Heifetz Ament – for their discerning appreciation of my creative activities over many decades, which provided me with ongoing encouragement.

Also, I have been privileged to benefit from the works of many people who filled my head and heart with the wonders of creativity. To name very few, authors Fyodor Dostoyevsky, Viktor E. Frankl, Anais Nin, Rainer M. Rilke; dancers Rudolph Nureyev, Wendy Whelan; painters Rembrandt, Soutine, Rothko; thinkers Sigmund Freud, Eric Kandel, Christopher Bollas, Martin Buber, Donald Winnicott, and Edith Kramer.

Profound thanks and gratitude to my family, my grandparents (especially my grandmother), parents and sisters; long-lived encouragement of friends, teachers and colleagues to follow my own inspiration; New York University for graduate study, requisite to entering psychoanalytic training, and to The Skirball Center at Temple E-Manuel for facilitating my study of Torah and biblical writings.

About the Author

Sandra Indig is a psychotherapist, artist, poet, dancer, and author. After undergraduate studies at the University of Michigan, she earned her BFA from Syracuse University. Sandra furthered her education at the New York University Graduate School of Social Work and the Washington Square Institute for Psychotherapy and Mental Health, and completed the internship in Art Therapy at Rikers Island.

Sandra is an active member of art societies, such as New York Artists' Circle, The American Alliance of Museums, and Jewish Art Salon. She had curated numerous exhibits, including three for the NYS Society for Clinical Social Work, and had been a recipient of multiple residences to art colonies: MacDowell Art Colony, New Hampshire; Virginia Center for the Creative Arts; and Vermont Studio Center. She was nominated twice for the Gradiva® Award in the category of Art by the National Association of the Advancement of Psychoanalysis (NAAP).

Sandra is a member of and has performed with the "Dances for a Variable Population" directed by Naomi Goldberg Haas. This company offers site-related public performances at many of NYC's most iconic spaces, such as Times Square, Washington Square Park, and Highline.

Sandra Indig's writing career started as a contributing writer for the Manhattan Arts International Magazine (Renee Phillips, editor), and it continued with *The Clinician and The Art League of Long Island*. Sandra's chapter, *Reclamation and Restoration: Heroes in the Seaweed*, is included in recently published Routledge book, *Art, Creativity, and Psychoanalysis: Artist / Analyst* (edited by George Hagman).

A seasoned clinician, Sandra Indig is an active member of the New York State Society for Clinical Social Work (NYSSCSW), where she had founded and serves as a chair of the Committee for Creativity & Neuro-Psycho-Education, and where she was honored for her contributions to the field of clinical social work.

She is also an international presenter and lecturer on creativity, creative process, psychoanalysis, and post-traumatic growth.

Sandra is in private practice in New York City, specializing in working with people living with creativity and recovery.

For examples of her art work and writing go to www.sindig.com.

CPSIA information can be obtained at www.ICGtesting.com
Printed in the USA
LVIW01n1902110117
520622LV00002B/2